Scott Foresman
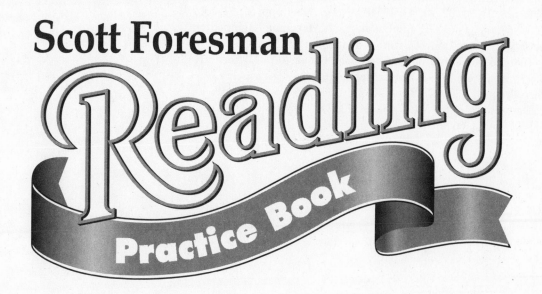
Reading

Practice Book

Scott Foresman

Editorial Offices: Glenview, Illinois • New York, New York
Sales Offices: Reading, Massachusetts • Duluth, Georgia • Glenview, Illinois
Carrollton, Texas • Menlo Park, California

Credits

Illustrations

Elizabeth Allen: pp. 83, 84, 85, 86, 87, 88; **Ellen Appleby:** pp. 9, 11, 15, 25, 26, 27, 31, 32, 41, 43, 47, 48; **Yvette Banek:** pp. 51, 52, 53, 54, 55, 56, 67, 68, 69, 71, 72; **Bill Basso:** p. 82; **Maryjane Begin:** cover; **Eldon Doty:** pp. 18, 91, 97; **Ruth J. Flanagan:** pp. 12, 28, 44, 76, 98–108; **Rachel Geswaldo:** p. 50; **Patrick Giouard:** p. 23; **Susan Hall:** pp. 13, 29, 45, 61, 77, 93; **Kersti Mack:** pp. 2, 34; **Patrick Merrell:** pp. 3, 4, 5, 6, 7, 8, 19, 20, 21, 22, 24, 35, 36, 37, 38, 39, 40, 42; **Doug Roy:** pp. 57, 58, 59, 60, 64, 73, 75, 79, 80, 84, 89, 92, 95, 96; **Joanna Roy:** p. 66

Editorial Offices
Glenview, Illinois • New York, New York

Sales Offices
Reading, Massachusetts • Duluth, Georgia • Glenview, Illinois
Carrollton, Texas • Menlo Park, California

ISBN 0-673-61110-8

7 8 9 10-CRK-06 05 04 03 02 01

Table of Contents

Family Times

A Real Gift

Arthur's Reading Race

Eat a Treat!

I stepped into my garden.
I saw a fuzzy peach.
I saw some peas and green beans.
They were within my reach.

I pulled off all the green beans.
I grabbed the pods with ease.
I picked the fuzzy big peach.
The peach was sure to please!

I made a little food stand.
I put out food to eat.
I wrote a sign for all to read
That listed every treat.

This rhyme includes words your child is working with at school: words with the long *e* sound spelled *ea* (*peach*) and words ending in *-ed* (*pulled*). Sing the rhyme together and act out the words.

(fold here)

Name: _____

You are your child's first and best teacher!

Here are ways to help your child practice skills while having fun!

Day 1 Say a word in which the long *e* sound is spelled *ea* as in *beat*. Encourage your child to say and spell a rhyming word that also uses the letters *ea*, such as *seat*. See how many pairs of words the two of you can name.

Day 2 Ask your child to make up a TV-commercial jingle, or song, that uses all of the following words: *buy, only, or, right,* and *think*. Help your child write the jingle.

Day 3 Play a prediction game with your child. Name an action or event, for example: *Two football teams arrive at a stadium.* Ask your child to tell what might happen next.

Day 4 Your child is learning about adjectives—words that describe people, places, and things. Name adjectives such as *happy, sad, angry,* or *silly,* and ask your child to draw faces to match these words.

Day 5 Help your child write about a favorite TV show or the characters on the show.

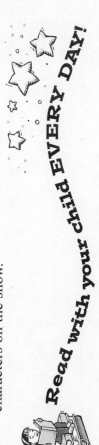

Read with your child EVERY DAY!

1

4

Verb Match Up

Materials   index cards, marker

Game Directions

1. Write each pair of verbs (with and without the -ed ending) on separate index cards.

2. Mix the cards and place each one facedown in rows and columns.

3. Players take turns turning over two cards at a time to match present and past tense verbs. If the cards match, player keeps the cards. If not, player returns cards to their original positions.

4. When all matches have been made, the player with the most pairs wins!

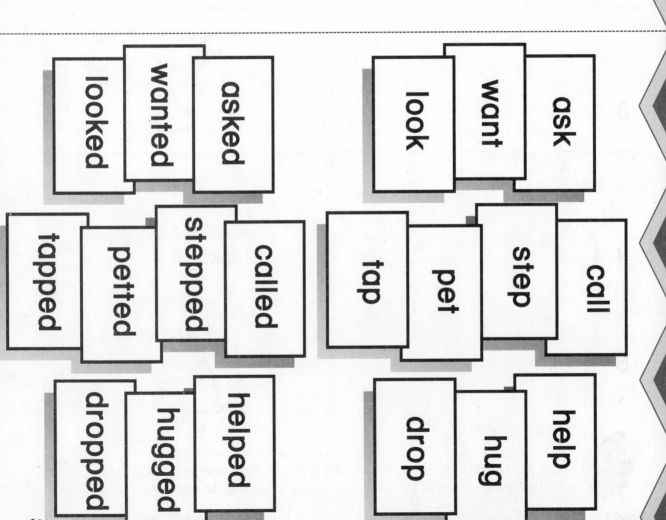

ask
want
look

call
step
pet
tap

help
hug
drop

asked
wanted
looked

called
stepped
petted
tapped

helped
hugged
dropped

Circle a word to finish each sentence.
Write it on the line.

p<u>ea</u>ch

read   red
_____
- - - - - - - - - - - -
1. I will _____ about a cat.

crate   cream
_____
- - - - - - - - - - - -
2. My cat likes _____ .

eat   ant
_____
- - - - - - - - - - - -
3. My cat likes to _____ .

tack   teach
_____
- - - - - - - - - - - -
4. I want to _____ my cat a trick.

flea   fun
_____
- - - - - - - - - - - -
5. The trick is _____ !

Notes for Home: Your child practiced reading words with the long *e* sound spelled *ea* as in
peach. **Home Activity:** Work with your child to make a list of other words with the long *e*
sound spelled *ea*. Ask your child to rhyme the new words with the words in these sentences.

Jan stepp**ed** on the box.
step + p + ed = stepped

Add -ed to each word.
Write the new word on the line.

1. clap _____

2. jump _____

3. stop _____

4. pet _____

5. ask _____

6. tug _____

7 call _____

8. rub _____

9. jog _____

10. hug _____

Notes for Home: Your child practiced writing words ending in *-ed*, like *stepped*.
Home Activity: Think of three or four verbs (for example: *pat*). Say each word aloud. Ask
your child to add *-ed* to each word, and then use each word in a sentence.

Name _____

Pick a word from the box to finish each sentence.
Write it on the line.

| buy | only | or | right | think |

1. Tom wants to _____ a hat.

2. He can get _____ one hat.

3. Will he get this hat _____ that one?

4. He has to _____ a bit.

5. This hat fits just _____ .

Notes for Home: This week your child is learning to read the words *buy, only, or, right,* and *think*. **Home Activity:** Write each word on a slip of paper. Put all the slips in a bowl or hat. Ask your child to pick a word, say it aloud, and use it in a sentence.

Name _____

Read the first sentence. Then **read** the pair of sentences.
Circle the sentence that tells what will happen next.
Draw a picture in the box that shows what will happen next.

1. Bob wakes up late.

   Bob will get to the bus on time.
   Bob will miss the bus.

2.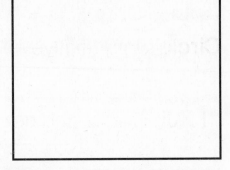

3. Mom and Dad pack for a trip.

   Mom and Dad will buy a dog.
   Mom and Dad will drive away.

4.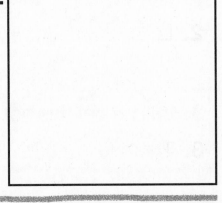

Look at the pictures.
Draw what will happen next.

5.

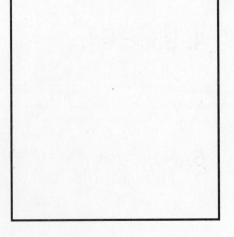

 Notes for Home: Your child predicted what will happen next in a story and drew a picture to show this prediction. **Home Activity:** Read a story to your child. At several points in the story, stop and ask your child to predict what will happen next.

Name _____

An **adjective** can tell about size, shape, color, or how many.
Big is an adjective.

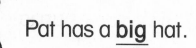

Pat has a **big** hat.

Circle the adjective in each sentence.

1. Jim has a long bat.

2. Look at the black cat.

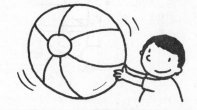

3. That's a huge ball.

4. Socks is a cute dog.

5. Pam has five hats.

Notes for Home: Your child identified adjectives that tell more about nouns—people, places, animals, or things. **Home Activity:** Look around the room. Point to an object and encourage your child to say an adjective that tells more about that object.

Level 1.5

Grammar: Adjectives (Describing Words) **7**

Pick a word from the box to match each clue.
Write the words in the puzzles.

buy   eight   only   or   right   think

1. Do you like cats _____ dogs?

2. not wrong

3. five, six, seven, _____

4. I have _____ one cat.

5. I _____ dogs are cute.

6. not sell

Notes for Home: Your child solved puzzles using words learned this week.
Home Activity: Work with your child to write a story using as many of these words as possible.

Name _____

Circle the word for each picture.

ph**o**ne

1. 	**2.** 	**3.** 	**4.** 
bone bun	ham home	note not	robe rob
5. 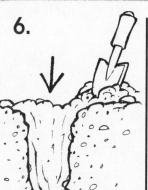	**6.** 	**7.** 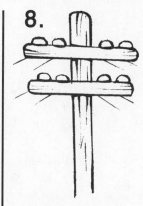	**8.**
knot nose	hold hole	rope ripe	pole pill

Find the word that has the same **long o** sound as .
Mark the ⬭ to show your answer.

9. ⬭ nod
   ⬭ rode
   ⬭ rod

10. ⬭ poke
    ⬭ dot
    ⬭ pot

 Notes for Home: Your child reviewed words with the long *o* sound that follow the pattern consonant-vowel-consonant-*e* (cone). ***Home Activity:*** Give a clue about each long *o* word shown above and challenge your child to guess it. For example: *What does a dog like to chew? (bone)*

Name _____

Look at each word. **Say** it.
Listen for the **-ed** ending.

	Write each word.	**Check** it.
1. ask		
2. call		
3. clean		
4. asked		
5. called		
6. cleaned		

Word Wall Words

Write each word.

7. think		
8. only		

Notes for Home: Your child spelled words with and without the ending -ed, as well as two frequently used words: *think, only*. **Home Activity:** Have your child use each spelling word in a sentence. Check that your child uses -ed words to describe actions in the past.

Pick the adjective from the box that matches each picture.
Write it on the line.

| sad | black | three | tall | small |

1. _____ man

2. _____ cat

3. _____ doll

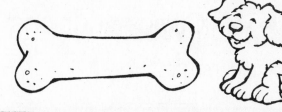

4. _____ dog

5. _____ ducks

Notes for Home: Your child used adjectives to describe objects. ***Home Activity:*** Say an adjective that describes color, shape, size, kind, or number *(white, round, small, happy,* or *five).* Have your child use that adjective to describe a person or object.

Name _____

Test-Taking Tips

1. Write your name on the test.

2. Read each question twice.

3. Read all the answer choices for the question.

4. Mark your answer carefully.

5. Check your answer.

Part 1: Vocabulary
Read each sentence.
Mark the ⬯ for the word that fits.

1. Dan wants to _____ a pet.
   ⬯ only   ⬯ buy   ⬯ sleep

2. There are _____ four pets here.
   ⬯ or   ⬯ out   ⬯ only

3. He has to _____ .
   ⬯ think   ⬯ right   ⬯ thank

4. Does he want a dog _____ a cat?
   ⬯ of   ⬯ or   ⬯ think

5. This cat is the _____ pet for Dan!
   ⬯ right   ⬯ buy   ⬯ more

GO ON

Part 2: Comprehension

Read each question.
Mark the ⬭ for the answer.

6. What does Arthur like to do?
   - ⬭ sing
   - ⬭ read
   - ⬭ sleep

7. If D.W. reads ten words, Arthur will
   - ⬭ give her a book.
   - ⬭ take her home.
   - ⬭ buy her an ice cream.

8. What is the first word D.W. reads?
   - ⬭ zoo
   - ⬭ gas
   - ⬭ walk

9. At the end of the story, D.W. sees that
   - ⬭ Arthur sat on wet paint.
   - ⬭ Arthur can't read his book.
   - ⬭ Arthur lost his ice cream.

10. What do you think D.W. will do on the way home?
    - ⬭ buy an ice cream for Arthur
    - ⬭ read something
    - ⬭ eat a hot dog

Name _____

Circle the compound word in each sentence.

strawberry

1. Jim swings by himself.

2. We played in the backyard.

3. Plants live everywhere.

4. We went inside.

5. Baseball is the best game!

6. Cupcakes are fun to bake.

7. I put on my bathrobe.

8. My friend has a ponytail.

Find the compound word.
Mark the ⬭ to show your answer.

9. ⬭ bathtub
   ⬭ bath
   ⬭ tube

10. ⬭ driver
    ⬭ dinner
    ⬭ driveway

Notes for Home: Your child reviewed compound words—words formed by joining two or more other words. **Home Activity:** Write words such as *out, side, in, any, thing, basket, ball, some, where,* and *one* on separate index cards. Have your child form compound words.

Name _____

| ask | call | clean | asked | called | cleaned |

Pick the pairs of words from the box that are alike.
Write the shorter word on the left.
Write the word **+ -ed** on the right.

<table>
<tr><th>Word</th><th>Word + -ed</th></tr>
</table>

Word _____   **Word + -ed** _____

1. _____   2. _____

3. _____   4. _____

5. _____   6. _____

Write the word from the box that rhymes with each word below.

_____   _____

7. mean _____   8. tall _____

Pick a word from the box that fits in each puzzle.
Write it in the puzzle.

| think | only |

9. | | | | | |

10. | | | | |

Notes for Home: Your child spelled words with and without the ending -ed, as well as two frequently used words: *think, only*. **Home Activity:** Say each spelling word. Ask your child to write it and use it in a sentence.

Family Times

Lost!

A Big Day for Jay

Oh, What a Day!

It's Saturday . . .
We swim all day . . .
We like to play . . .
Down by the bay . . . .

It starts to rain . . .
And we can't stay . . .
We waddle home . . .
But lose our way . . . .

A kind gray snail . . .
Shows us the way . . .
We'll soon be home . . . .
Oh, what a day!

This rhyme includes words your child is working with at school: words with the long *a* sound spelled *ay* and *ai* (*play*, *rain*) and contractions (*We'll*). Read aloud "Oh, What a Day!" together. Think up more words that rhyme with the long *a* words in this rhyme.

(fold here)

Name: _____

You are your child's first and best teacher!

Here are ways to help your child practice skills while having fun!

Day 1 Write a simple sentence using two words that can be made into a contraction, such as *She is at home*. Ask your child to rewrite the sentence using a contraction: *She's at home.*

Day 2 Write simple sentences using these words: *don't, from, hear, live,* and *when*. Help your child read each sentence.

Day 3 Look for pictures of two similar objects in a catalog. Ask your child to point out things that are different and things that are alike in the two pictures.

Day 4 Your child is learning about solving problems. Present your child with a problem situation and ask: *What would you do if that happened to you?*

Day 5 Look at newspapers with your child. Then encourage him or her to make up a news story about a child or animal who gets lost. Work together to write the story.

Read with your child EVERY DAY!

4

Name a Rhyme

Materials paper, 1 coin

Game Directions

1. Players take turns tossing a coin onto the gameboard and reading the word that the coin lands on.

2. A player earns a point for each rhyming word named that spells the long *a* sound the same way as the word landed on. Make a list of the words used. Do not use a word more than once. Possible rhyming words are given below.

3. The first player to get 15 points wins!

Rhyming Words:
snail, pail, mail, trail, fail, jail; hay, play, day, way, bay, stay, away; rain, train, drain, sprain, brain, main

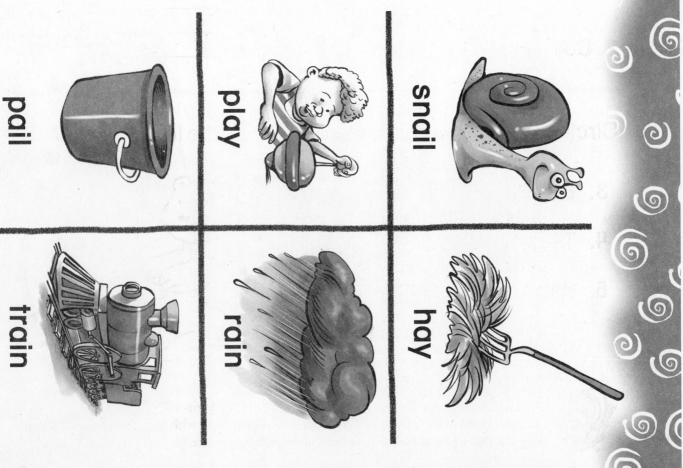

snail

hay

play

rain

pail

train

Name _____

Write the word for each picture.

n<u>ai</u>l   h<u>ay</u>

_____   _____

1. Put the _____ in the _____ .

_____   _____

2. Does a _____ have a _____ ?

Circle the word in each sentence that has the **long a** sound.

3. Ben likes to play.

4. The ball blows away.

5. Which way did it go?

Notes for Home: Your child practiced writing and reading words with the long *a* sound spelled *ai* (as in *nail*) and *ay* (as in *hay*). **Home Activity:** Work with your child to write a short story using as many of the long *a* words on the page as possible.

© Scott Foresman   1

Name _____

Pick a word from the box that means the same as each pair of words.
Write it on the line.

She is tall.
She's tall.

| you'll | it's | that's | aren't |
| I'll | I'm | hadn't | don't |

1. it + is

_____

- - - - - - - - - - -

_____

2. that + is

_____

- - - - - - - - - - -

_____

3. are + not

_____

- - - - - - - - - - -

_____

4. you + will

_____

- - - - - - - - - - -

_____

5. I + will

_____

- - - - - - - - - - -

_____

6. I + am

_____

- - - - - - - - - - -

_____

7. do + not

_____

- - - - - - - - - - -

_____

8. had + not

_____

- - - - - - - - - - -

_____

Notes for Home: Your child learned to identify and write contractions, such as *I'll* and *She's*.
Home Activity: Read each contraction on this page aloud. Challenge your child to use each
one in a sentence. Work together to write each in a sentence.

Name _____

Pick a word from the box to finish each sentence.
Write it on the line.

don't	from	hear	live	when

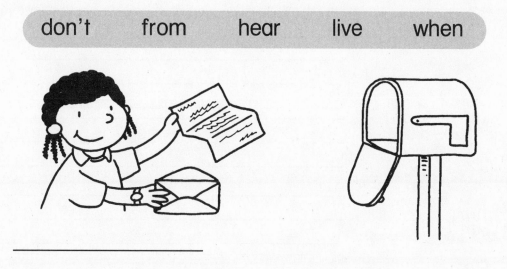

1. I _____ the mail truck beep.

2. I got a note _____ my friend.

3. My friend used to _____ here.

4. Now I _____ see him anymore.

5. I am glad _____ he writes to me!

Notes for Home: This week your child is learning to read the words *don't, from, hear, live,* and *when.* **Home Activity:** Encourage your child to tell you a story using these words. Make a picture book of the completed story. Help your child write a caption for each picture.

Name _____

Look at both pictures.
Write sentences to tell how the pictures are the same and different.

Same

_____

1. _____

_____

2. _____

_____

Pip

Different

_____

3. _____

_____

4. _____

_____

Rex

5. _____

_____

Notes for Home: Your child used pictures to tell how two things are alike and different.
Home Activity: Point out two objects to your child. Encourage your child to tell you how they
are the same and how they are different.

Name _____

An **adjective** can tell what color or what shape something is.

The box is **square**.

Circle the adjective in each sentence.
Color the picture to match the adjectives.

1. The ball is blue.

2. The clown has red hair.

3. He has a purple hat.

Draw a picture for each group of words.

| 4. a square clock | 5. a wide river |

Notes for Home: Your child identified adjectives for colors and shapes. *Home Activity:* Name a color or shape. Ask your child to point out an object that has that color or shape.

© Scott Foresman 1

Name _____

Pick a word from the box to finish each sentence.
Write it on the line.

don't	from	hear	hurt	live	when

1. I _____ a pup.

2. Are you _____ , pup?

3. You _____ look hurt.

4. Where do you _____ ?

5. You are not _____ this block.

6. You will be glad _____ I find your home.

Notes for Home: Your child used new vocabulary words to complete a story. ***Home Activity:***
Read the vocabulary words aloud. Ask your child to write each word and explain its meaning.

24 **Vocabulary/High-Frequency Words**

Level 1.5

Name _____

 r**a**ke   P**e**te    b**i**ke   h**o**me   c**u**be

Circle the word for each picture.

1. 	2. 	3. 	4. 
spice space	kite kit	cane can	rose rise

5. 	6. 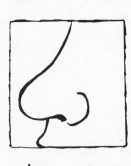	7. 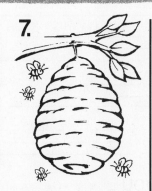	8. 
get gate	nice nose	hive have	tub tube

Find the word that has the **long vowel** sound.
Mark the ⬭ to show your answer.

9. ⬭ late
   ⬭ plan
   ⬭ man

10. ⬭ bite
    ⬭ bit
    ⬭ brick

 Notes for Home: Your child reviewed long vowel sounds in words ending with *e*. **Home Activity:** Write the words *Tim*, *rat*, *kit*, *can*, *rid*, and *rob* on a piece of paper. Ask your child to say each word. Then add *e* to the end of each word. Ask your child to say each new word.

© Scott Foresman 1

Name _____

Look at each word. **Say** it.
Listen for the **long a** sound in

Write each word.   **Check** it.

1. say

2. play

3. may

4. way

5. wait

6. rain

Word Wall Words

Write each word.

7. when

8. from

Notes for Home: Your child spelled words in which the long *a* sound is spelled *ai* and *ay* and two frequently used words: *when, from.* **Home Activity:** Say each spelling word. Ask your child to spell the word, and then use it in a sentence. Together, draw pictures for the sentences.

Follow the directions.
Then, **pick** the best adjective
from the box to finish each sentence.
Write it on the line.

> square   round   green   red   yellow

1. Color the hat green.

   _____
   - - - - - - - - - - - - - -
   This is a _____ hat.

2. Draw a round stone.

   _____
   - - - - - - - - - - - - - -
   This is a _____ stone.

3. Color the chick yellow.

   _____
   - - - - - - - - - - - - - -
   This is a _____ chick.

4. Draw a square box.

   _____
   - - - - - - - - - - - - - -
   This is a _____ box.

5. Color the fish red.

   _____
   - - - - - - - - - - - - - -
   This is a _____ fish.

Notes for Home: Your child used adjectives to describe color and shape. *Home Activity:* Encourage your child to draw pictures showing objects of different colors and shapes. Work with your child to label each picture, for example, *a blue bear.*

Test-Taking Tips

1. Write your name on the test.

2. Read each question twice.

3. Read all the answer choices for the question.

4. Mark your answer carefully.

5. Check your answer.

© Scott Foresman 1

Part I: Vocabulary

Read each sentence.
Mark the ⬭ for the word that fits.

1. I _____ something crying.
   ⬭ hear   ⬭ buy   ⬭ live

2. I cannot see what it is _____ here.
   ⬭ don't   ⬭ why   ⬭ from

3. _____ I go out, I see it.
   ⬭ For   ⬭ When   ⬭ Want

4. "_____ be sad," I say.
   ⬭ Down   ⬭ From   ⬭ Don't

5. "I think you _____ here."
   ⬭ live   ⬭ bring   ⬭ think

© Scott Foresman 1

Part 2: Comprehension

Read each question.
Mark the ⬭ for the answer.

6. What does the bear want to find?
   - ⬭ some buildings
   - ⬭ a library
   - ⬭ his home

7. From the top of a building, he sees
   - ⬭ trees and water.
   - ⬭ friends.
   - ⬭ more bears.

8. What does the bear do in the park?
   - ⬭ read
   - ⬭ eat
   - ⬭ sleep

9. They go to the library to
   - ⬭ find out where the bear lives.
   - ⬭ have a good time.
   - ⬭ go for a bus ride.

10. How are the bear and his friend alike?
    - ⬭ They both sleep on the bus.
    - ⬭ They both get lost.
    - ⬭ They both like trucks.

STOP

Name _____

 **ch**est    **sh**op    **th**in   **wh**istle

Circle the word for each picture.

1. 	2. 	3. 	4. 
sheep deep	gale whale	heat wheat	thorn torn

5. 	6. 	7. 	8. 
ship whip	there chair	thick chick	sell shell

Find the word that has the same beginning sound as .
Mark the ⬭ to show your answer.

9. ⬭ cheap
⬭ keep
⬭ care

10. ⬭ cold
⬭ calm
⬭ child

 Notes for Home: Your child reviewed digraphs—two letters that represent one sound—as in *chest*, *shop*, *thin*, and *whistle*. **Home Activity:** Together, write words beginning with *ch, sh, th,* and *wh* that have the same beginning sounds as the words shown above.

Level 1.5

Phonics: Initial Digraphs *ch, sh, th, wh* **Review 31**

© Scott Foresman 1

Name _____

| say | play | may | way | wait | rain |

Write four words from the box that rhyme with **day**.

1. _____

2. _____

3. _____

4. _____

Write the word from the box that rhymes with each word below.

5. bait _____

6. main _____

Pick a word from the box to finish each sentence.
Write it on the line.

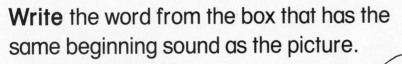

7. We like to _____ games.

8. _____ for me to hide.

Write the word from the box that has the same beginning sound as the picture.

| when | from |

9.  _____

10. _____

Notes for Home: Your child spelled words in which the long *a* sound is spelled *ai* and *ay*, as well as two frequently used words: *when, from.* **Home Activity:** Challenge your child to write other words with *ai* and *ay* that have a long *a* sound.

32 Spelling: Long *a: ai, ay*

Level 1.5

© Scott Foresman 1

Family Times

Baby Otter Grows Up

Foal

I See a Foal

I see a foal with a shiny coat.
I see a foal playing with a goat.

I see a foal roaming all around.
I see a foal jumping on the ground.

I see a foal looking at a crow.
I see a foal running in the snow.

This rhyme includes words your child is working with in school: words with the long *o* sound spelled *oa* and *ow* (*foal, crow*) and words that end in *-ing* (*playing*). Sing "I See a Foal" with your child. Have your child act out the parts of the foal.

(fold here)

Name: _____

You are your child's first and best teacher!

Here are ways to help your child practice skills while having fun!

Day 1 Act out words that end with *-ing*, such as *running, jumping, hopping,* and *eating.* See if your child can guess which word you are acting out.

Day 2 Encourage your child to make up sentences that include the following words children are learning to read this week: *around, her, new, old,* and *show.*

Day 3 Write the events of a familiar story, but put the events out of order. Ask your child to retell the story with the events in the proper order.

Day 4 Your child is learning to identify the main idea in a story. Read a story aloud to your child. Then ask your child to write a sentence or two telling what the story was all about.

Day 5 Go for a walk with your child. Point out objects or people along the way and ask your child to describe them using an adjective for size, such as a *small* dog or a *big* truck.

Read with your child EVERY DAY!

Spin and Spell

Materials paper, scissors, paper clip, pencil, 1 button per player

Game Directions

1. Make a simple spinner as shown.

2. Players take turns spinning and then naming and spelling a word with the long *o* sound spelled either *oa* as in *boat* or *ow* as in *row*. Words that could be used include: *boat, coat, soap, foal, goat, row, crow, grow, know, blow.*

3. If a player spells the word correctly, he or she moves that number of spaces.

4. The first player to reach the end wins!

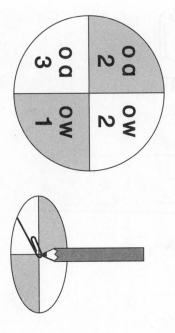

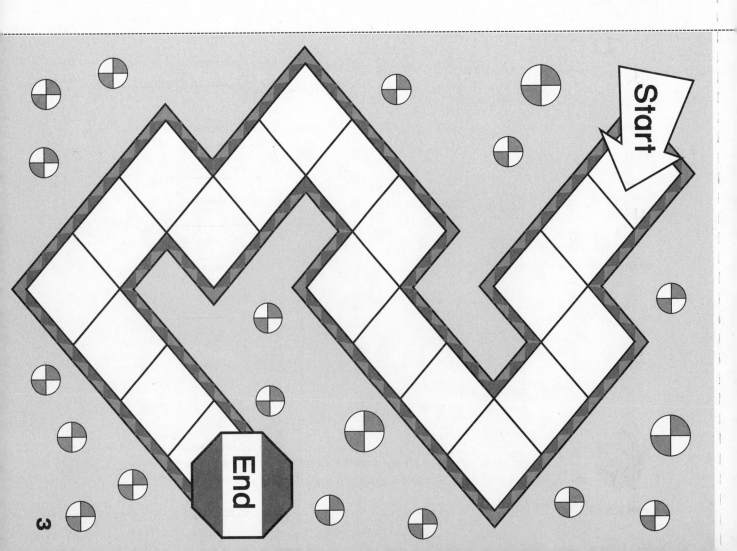

Circle the word for each picture.
Write it on the line.

 c**oa**t   wind**ow**

1. bat _____
   boat - - - - - -
   beet _____

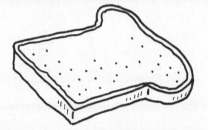

2. toast _____
   tea - - - - - -
   top _____

3. road _____
   run - - - - - -
   red _____

4. crop _____
   cap - - - - - -
   crow _____

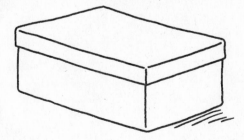

5. bill _____
   bowl - - - - - -
   box _____

Notes for Home: Your child practiced reading words with the long *o* sound spelled *oa* (as in *coat*) and *ow* (as in *window*). **Home Activity:** Read each long *o* word on this page aloud. Encourage your child to think of a word that rhymes with each word.

Name _____

Pick a word from the box that tells what each person is doing.
Write it on the line.

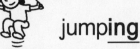

| eating   running   sitting | jump**ing** |

Alex

_____
1. Alex is _____ .

Terry

_____
2. Terry is _____ .

Pat

_____
3. Pat is _____ .

Draw a picture to show each action.

4. reading

5. barking

Notes for Home: Your child read words ending in *-ing*, such as *jumping*. **Home Activity:** Encourage your child to point out verbs with *-ing* as you read together. Have your child say the verb with and without *-ing*.

36   **Phonics: Inflected Ending** *-ing*

Level 1.5

Name _____

Pick a word from the box to match each clue.
Write the words in the puzzles.

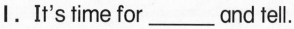

around   her   new   old   show

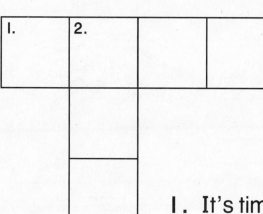

1. It's time for _____ and tell.

2. Kim holds _____ rabbit.

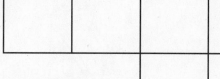

3. The top spins _____ .

4. not new

5. not old

Notes for Home: This week your child is learning to read the words *around, her, new, old,* and *show.* **Home Activity:** Encourage your child to make up a story or poem using these vocabulary words. Work together to write the story or poem and read it to other family members or friends.

Level 1.5

Look at the pictures.
Write I, 2, 3 to put the sentences in order.

_____
- - - - - - - -

1. Then Dan picked a puppy. _____

_____
- - - - - - - -

2. Dan played with his new puppy at home. _____

_____
- - - - - - - -

3. Dan and his mother went to the pet store. _____

_____
- - - - - - - -

4. Jen and Sam went home. _____

_____
- - - - - - - -

5. First Jen and Sam went to the park. _____

_____
- - - - - - - -

6. Jen and Sam played on the slide. _____

 Notes for Home: Your child put a sequence of events in order to form a story. ***Home Activity:*** Ask your child to draw a series of pictures showing three events in the order in which they happened.

Name _____

An **adjective** can tell what size something is.

The <u>small</u> pup is in a **big** box.

Pick a word from the box to finish each sentence.
Write it on the line.

| big | short | small | long | tiny |

1. Ben has a _____ string.

2. Jill has a _____ string.

3. Tom has a _____ box.

4. Jill has a _____ box.

5. The cats are _____ .

 Notes for Home: Your child identified adjectives for sizes, such as *big* and *tiny*. **Home Activity:** Say each adjective in the box above. Encourage your child to use that adjective to describe something else.

Pick a word from the box to finish each sentence.
Write it on the line.

around   her   new   old   ponies   show

_____
- -
1. Look at the _____ .

_____
- -
2. One pony has a _____ baby foal.

_____
- -
3. The foal looks _____ for its mother.

_____
- -
4. The mother is close to _____ foal.

_____
- -
5. The foal is new, but the mother is _____ .

_____
- -
6. I want to _____ the foal to my dad!

Notes for Home: Your child used newly learned words to finish a story. **Home Activity:** Spell each of the vocabulary words aloud. Ask your child to name each word.

 m**e**    w**ee**k   b**ea**n

Say the word for each picture.
Write e, **ee**, or **ea** to finish each word.

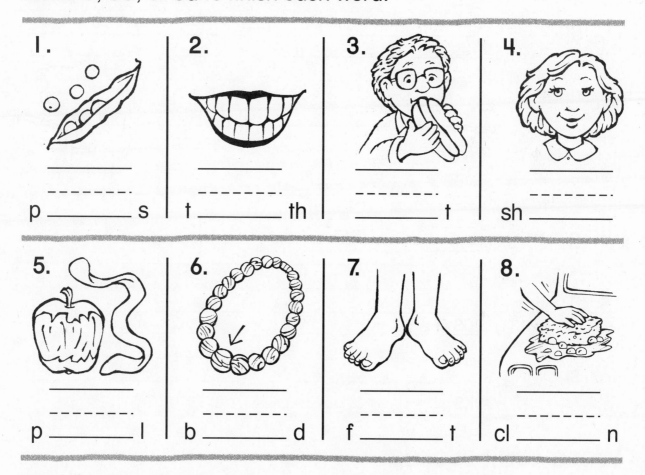

1. _____ p _____ s

2. _____ t _____ th

3. _____ t

4. _____ sh _____

5. _____ p _____ l

6. _____ b _____ d

7. _____ f _____ t

8. _____ cl _____ n

Find the word that has the same **long e** sound as **bee**.
Mark the ⬭ to show your answer.

9. ⬭ we
    ⬭ wet
    ⬭ white

10. ⬭ ten
     ⬭ tent
     ⬭ tea

 Notes for Home: Your child reviewed words in which the long *e* sound is spelled *e, ee,* and *ea.*
Home Activity: Ask your child to think of a rhyming word for each long *e* word on this page.
Write the words and look at how the vowel sound is spelled.

Name _____

Look at each word. **Say** it.
Listen for the **long o** sound in  .

Write each word.	**Check** it.

1. grow

2. float

3. show

4. growing

5. floating

6. showing

Word Wall Words

Write each word.

7. around

8. old

Notes for Home: Your child spelled words with and without the ending -ing, and two frequently used words: *around, old*. **Home Activity:** Challenge your child to add -ing to other action words such as *jump, look, see,* and *help*.

© Scott Foresman 1

Follow the directions.
Then, **pick** the best adjective from
the box to finish each sentence.
Write it on the line. Use each word only once.

| thin | long | big | fat | little |

1. Color the big dog.

   _____
   - - - - - - - - - -
   Rover is a _____ dog.

2. Color the long rope.

   _____
   - - - - - - - - - -
   The _____ rope has a knot.

3. Color in the paws on the little pup.

   _____
   - - - - - - - - - -
   Boots is a _____ pup.

4. Draw a hat on a fat cat.

   _____
   - - - - - - - - - -
   This _____ cat has a hat.

5. Circle the thin line.

   _____
   - - - - - - - - - -
   This line is _____ .

Notes for Home: Your child used adjectives to describe size. ***Home Activity:*** Go for a walk with your child. Encourage him or her to describe the objects and people you see using size adjectives, such as *big, small, tall,* and *short, huge, tiny.*

Test-Taking Tips

1. Write your name on the test.

2. Read each question twice.

3. Read all the answer choices for the question.

4. Mark your answer carefully.

5. Check your answer.

Name _____

Part 1: Vocabulary

Read each sentence.
Mark the ⬭ for the word that fits.

1. Jen has a _____ friend.
   ⬭ how   ⬭ down   ⬭ new

2. Jen and Anna run _____ the tree.
   ⬭ around   ⬭ old   ⬭ with

3. Anna wants to _____ Jen something.
   ⬭ catch   ⬭ hold   ⬭ show

4. Look who is in _____ house!
   ⬭ any   ⬭ her   ⬭ new

5. He is only five days _____ .
   ⬭ old   ⬭ or   ⬭ around

Part 2: Comprehension

Read each question.
Mark the ⊂⊃ for the answer.

6. What does a foal eat when it is new?
   - ⊂⊃ grass
   - ⊂⊃ milk
   - ⊂⊃ apples

7. What does the foal get when it is two weeks old?
   - ⊂⊃ a new home
   - ⊂⊃ a friend
   - ⊂⊃ two new teeth

8. When the foal wants its mother, it
   - ⊂⊃ runs around the field.
   - ⊂⊃ neighs loudly.
   - ⊂⊃ eats red apples.

9. The foal is nearly full-grown at
   - ⊂⊃ one week.
   - ⊂⊃ five weeks.
   - ⊂⊃ five months.

10. You can tell that new foals
    - ⊂⊃ are not very happy.
    - ⊂⊃ eat what you eat.
    - ⊂⊃ grow fast.

STOP

Name _____

Pick a letter or letters to finish each word.
Write the letters on the lines.

| bb | d | g | m | pp | rr | tt | z |

ki<u>tt</u>en   ze<u>b</u>ra

1.

o _____ er

2.

ti _____ er

3.

spi _____ er

4.
ra _____ it

5.

pu _____ y

6.

ca _____ el

7.

pa _____ ot

8.

li _____ ard

Find the word that has the same middle consonant sound as the picture.
Mark the ⬭ to show your answer.

9. ⬭ button
⬭ kidding
⬭ muffin

10. ⬭ rice
⬭ never
⬭ rider

Notes for Home: Your child completed words with two syllables that have single or double consonants in the middle, such as *kitten* and *zebra*. **Home Activity:** Help your child name things around your home that have consonants in the middle (*sofa*, *radio*, *letters*, *pillows*, *papers*).

| grow | float | show | growing | floating | showing |

Pick the pairs of words from the box that are alike.
Write the shorter word on the left.
Write the word + **-ing** on the right.

Word	**Word + -ing**
_____	_____
1. _____	2. _____
_____	_____
3. _____	4. _____
_____	_____
5. _____	6. _____

Pick a word from the box to finish each sentence.
Write the word in the puzzle.

| around | old |

7. Rex is an _____ dog.

8. He likes to walk _____ the block.

Notes for Home: Your child spelled words with and without the ending *-ing*, and two frequently used words: *around, old.* **Home Activity:** Ask your child to use each spelling word in a sentence. Help your child write the sentences.

Family Times

What a Sight

Lost in the Museum

Dwight the Knight

There was a boy named Dwight.
Dwight's school was a delight.
Dwight's class had gone to see some sights
Like kings and queens and knights.

When Dwight went home that night,
He dreamed he was a knight.
Dwight's horse was big.
Dwight's sword was light.
Dwight's armor shined so bright.

This rhyme includes words your child is working with in school: words with long i spelled igh (night) and words that are possessives (Dwight's). Sing "Dwight the Knight" with your child. Then underline the long i words and circle the possessives.

(fold here)

Name: _____

You are your child's first and best teacher!

Here are ways to help your child practice skills while having fun!

Day 1 Your child is learning to use possessives—words that show ownership. Encourage your child to make up a funny story using as many possessives as possible, such as *Mom's* and *Dad's*.

Day 2 Your child is learning to read these words: *been, first, found, start,* and *together*. Ask your child to cut letters out of magazines or newspapers to spell these words.

Day 3 Help your child draw a set of two pictures that shows what happens (effect) and why it happens (cause), such as a flat bike tire (effect) and a nail in the road (cause).

Day 4 Create a simple graphic organizer with your child. Write a noun such as *dog* inside a circle, and ask your child to write words that might describe that noun around the outside of the center circle.

Day 5 Name an adjective that tells what kind something is, such as *hot, wet,* or *sad*. Ask your child to say the adjective that is the opposite of the one you named.

Read with your child EVERY DAY!

4

Phonics Dominoes

Materials   index cards, marker, ruler

Game Directions

1. Use the long *i* words below to make dominoes like those shown on page 3. Write pairs of words on index cards. Words can be used more than once, but not on the same domino.

2. Shuffle the dominoes, place them facedown, and have each player select six.

3. Players take turns lining up the dominoes to match words with *igh* or words with *ie*. See the example on page 3. If a play is not possible, player must draw a domino from the pile.

4. The first player to use all his or her dominoes wins!

Long *i* Words

high	night	flight	pie
bright	right	fight	lie
tight	might	sight	die
sigh	light	fright	tie

flight	
fright	right
night	lie
sigh	pie
tie	might

2

3

Name _____

Pick a word from the box to finish each sentence.
Write it on the line.

| fright | light | night | pie | right |

I eat p**ie** at n**igh**t.

1. I had a dream last _____ .

2. There was something bad in my _____ .

3. It gave me such a _____ !

4. I woke up and put on the _____ .

5. Then I was all _____ .

Notes for Home: Your child practiced reading words with the long *i* sound spelled *ie (pie)* and *igh (night)*. **Home Activity:** Read the long *i* words on this page aloud. Ask your child to think of a word that rhymes with each word.

Name _____

Add 's to the end of each word.
Write the new word on the line.

Meg's hat

---

1. Jim ⎯⎯ bat

2. baby ⎯⎯ laugh

3. Max ⎯⎯ book

4. Kate ⎯⎯ kite

5. Mom ⎯⎯ cup

6. boy ⎯⎯ games

7. Ben ⎯⎯ cat

8. Jill ⎯⎯ horn

Pick a word from the box to match each picture.
Write it on the line.

Jen's   Matt's

9. ⎯⎯⎯⎯ hat

---

10. ⎯⎯⎯⎯ ball

Notes for Home: Your child wrote words with *'s* to show ownership. *Home Activity:* Point out objects in your home or outside that are owned by one person. Ask your child to use a possessive to tell you who owns each object *(Mike's bike)*.

Pick a word from the box to finish each sentence.
Write it on the line. Use each word only once.

been	first	found	start	together

1. We went to the store _____ .

2. _____ we went to buy fish.

3. My mother got lost.

   I had to _____ yelling.

4. Then I saw her.

   She had _____ looking for me.

5. I was glad I _____ her!

Notes for Home: This week your child is learning the words *been, first, found, start,* and *together.* **Home Activity:** Use each of these words in a simple sentence. Help your child read each sentence aloud.

Name _____

Draw a line to match what happens with why it happens.

What Happens	**Why It Happens**

1.

2.

3.

4.

 Notes for Home: Your child connected pictures to show what happens (effect) and why it happens (cause). **Home Activity:** Describe an event to your child (For example: *A cat jumps onto a shelf full of glasses.*). Encourage your child to tell you what might happen next.

Level 1.5

Name _____

Some **adjectives** tell what kind.
Wet tells what kind of day it is.

It is a <u>**wet**</u> day.

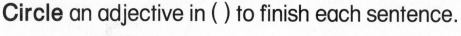

Circle an adjective in ( ) to finish each sentence.

1. This is a (funny / yummy) cake.

2. What a (hard / soft) bed!

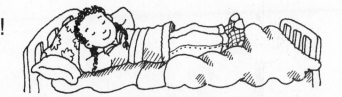

3. The dog is (wet / dry) .

4. He has a (neat / messy) place.

5. I read a (sad / funny) book.

Notes for Home: Your child identified adjectives that tell what kind, such as *wet* or *soft*.
Home Activity: Point out objects to your child. Encourage your child to name an adjective
telling what kind of object each one is.

Pick a word from the box that is the opposite of each word below.
Write it on the line.

| been | first | found | start | together |

1. stop

_____

2. last

_____

3. lost

_____

4. apart

_____

Write a sentence with the word *been*.

5. _____

_____

Notes for Home: Your child identified opposites and wrote a sentence using words learned this week. ***Home Activity:*** Encourage your child to make up a song or poem using as many of these words as possible.

© Scott Foresman 1

Name _____

Look at the map.
Write the answer to each question.

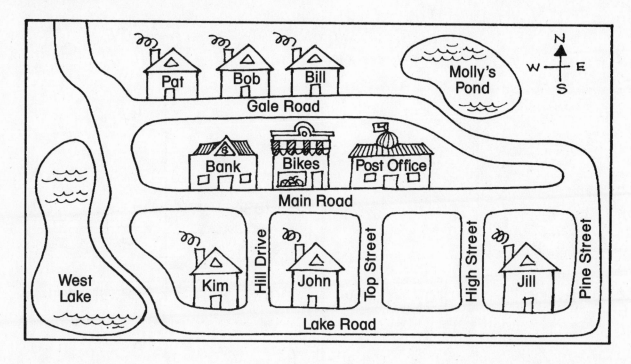

_____
- - - - - - - - - - - - - - - - -

1. What road does Bob live on? _____

_____

2. What road is the bike shop on? _____

- - - - - - - - - - - -

3. Who lives closer to West Lake, Kim or Jill? _____

- - - - - - - - - -

4. What road would Jill take to get to Kim's home quickly?

_____
- -
_____

 Notes for Home: Your child read a map and answered questions about it. **Home Activity:** Look at a map of your town with your child. Go over the different symbols and explain what they mean. Then point out two places and ask him or her to show you how to get from one place to the other.

Name _____

t<u>ai</u>l

 play

Circle the word for each picture.

1.

pal   pail

2.

gray   grow

3.

pan   pain

4.

sell   sail

5.

mail   mill

6.

he   hay

7.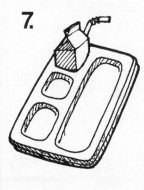

tray   tree

8.

bay   bow

Find the word that has the same **long a** sound as .
Mark the  to show your answer.

9. ⬭ rap
   ⬭ clap
   ⬭ clay

10. ⬭ nap
    ⬭ neat
    ⬭ nail

 Notes for Home: Your child reviewed words in which the long *a* sound is spelled *ai* and *ay*.
Home Activity: Ask your child to think of a rhyming word for each long *a* word on this page.

Name _____

Look at each word. **Say** it.
Listen for the **long i** sound in  .

Write each word.   **Check** it.

1. lie _____   _____

2. pie _____   _____

3. tie _____   _____

4. night _____   _____

5. light _____   _____

6. right _____   _____

Word Wall Words

Write each word.

7. been _____   _____

8. found _____   _____

Notes for Home: Your child spelled words with the long *i* sound spelled *ie* and *igh*, and two frequently used words: *been, found.* **Home Activity:** Work with your child to write a story that includes the spelling words about getting lost in a bakery.

Name _____

Pick the best adjective from the box to finish each sentence.
Write it on the line.

soft	clean	wet	old	full

1. This is a _____ box.

2. This is an _____ home.

3. This kitten is _____ .

4. The _____ dog shakes.

5. I need a _____ dish to use.

Notes for Home: Your child used adjectives that tell what kind of object something is, such as *full box* or *wet dog*. **Home Activity:** Play *I Spy* with your child. Encourage your child to describe an object using adjectives for kind, and see if you can guess what object he or she is talking about.

60 **Grammar: Adjectives for Kinds**

Level 1.5

Name _____

Part 1: Vocabulary
Read each sentence.
Mark the ⬭ for the word that fits.

1. Have you _____ to the sea?
  ⬭ been   ⬭ found   ⬭ done

2. Dean and Pam run _____ .
  ⬭ lost   ⬭ something   ⬭ together

3. Pam was the _____ one in the water.
  ⬭ any   ⬭ first   ⬭ together

4. Dean _____ a pretty shell.
  ⬭ said   ⬭ found   ⬭ went

5. Soon it was time to _____ for home.
  ⬭ start   ⬭ hold   ⬭ bring

 GO ON ➡

© Scott Foresman 1

Part 2: Comprehension

Read each question.

Mark the ⬭ for the answer.

6. The teacher wants everyone to
   - ⬭ stay together.
   - ⬭ get lost.
   - ⬭ see the dinosaur.

7. Why does Jim go with Danny?
   - ⬭ He does not hear the teacher.
   - ⬭ He wants to see a dinosaur.
   - ⬭ The teacher tells him to go.

8. Jim runs away from the dinosaur because he
   - ⬭ wants to eat hot dogs.
   - ⬭ is scared.
   - ⬭ does not want to get lost.

9. Jim is brave when he
   - ⬭ sees the dinosaur.
   - ⬭ goes to find his teacher.
   - ⬭ eats a hot dog.

10. How does Jim find his teacher?
    - ⬭ He asks the whale for help.
    - ⬭ The penguins tell him what to do.
    - ⬭ He looks in many rooms.

Write the contraction for each pair of words.

1. I + am = _____

2. you + will = _____

3. will + not = _____

4. they + are = _____

5. could + not = _____

6. she + had = _____

7. do + not = _____

8. would + not = _____

Find the contraction.
Mark the ⬭ to show your answer.

9. ⬭ it's
   ⬭ hits
   ⬭ its

10. ⬭ were
    ⬭ we're
    ⬭ worry

Notes for Home: Your child reviewed contractions—words made up of two words and an apostrophe. *Home Activity:* Write the words *it, is, did, not, I, am, we,* and *are* on separate index cards. Ask your child to see how many different contractions he or she can form.

lie   pie   tie   night   light   right

Write three words from the box that rhyme with **my**.

1. _____ 2. _____ 3. _____

Write three words from the box that rhyme with **fight**.

4. _____ 5. _____ 6. _____

Pick a word from the box to finish each sentence.
Write it on the line.

7. I won't tell a _____ .

8. I ate the _____ .

Pick a word from the box to finish each sentence.
Write it on the line.

been   found

9. I have _____ at Fred's shop.

10. I _____ two cats there!

 Notes for Home: Your child spelled words with the long *i* sound spelled *ie* and *igh*. **Home Activity:** Ask your child to make up a silly song using the spelling words. Work together to write the words to the song when it's finished.

Family Times

Chompy's Afternoon

Dinosaur Babies

I'm a Baby Dinosaur

I'm a baby dinosaur.
I hatched from my own eggshell.
I'm hungry for my breakfast now.
I want the berry I smell!

I'm a baby dinosaur
With footprints that are tiny.
My head and mouth are very large.
My teeth are big and shiny.

This rhyme includes words your child is working with in school: words with *y* that represent the long *e* sound (*hungry*) and the long *i* sound (*my*) as well as compound words (*eggshell*). Chant "I'm a Baby Dinosaur" with your child. Sort all the words with *y* into two groups according to the two different vowel sounds.

(fold here)

Name: _____

You are your child's first and best teacher!

Here are ways to help your child practice skills while having fun!

Day 1 Work with your child to think of pairs of words that have the long *e* and long *i* vowel sounds of *y*, such as *pretty city*; *funny baby*; *shy fly*; or *dry sky*.

Day 2 Make up a simple crossword or word search puzzle using the following words that the children are learning to read: *animals*, *even*, *heard*, *most*, and *their*.

Day 3 Read a paragraph from a children's story or magazine article to your child. Ask him or her to tell you what the main idea of the paragraph is.

Day 4 Ask your child to choose a topic he or she is interested in, such as a favorite animal or sports figure, and to present an oral report about that topic to the family. Encourage your child to speak clearly.

Day 5 Play "I Spy" with your child using number adjectives. For example, you might see two books and say *I spy some books. Tell me how many.* Your child must then name and spell the appropriate number (*two*).

Read with your child EVERY DAY!

Compound Treasures

Materials paper, marker, scissors, paper clip, pencil, 1 button per player

Game Directions

1. Make a simple spinner as shown.

2. Players place buttons on Start, take turns spinning, and move the number of spaces shown.

3. When a player lands on a picture square, he or she must say the compound word that names the picture. Answers are shown below.

4. The first player to reach the end wins!

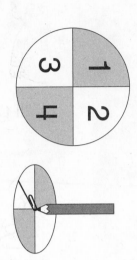

Answers (in order): football, eggshell, raincoat, cowboy, footprint, cupcake

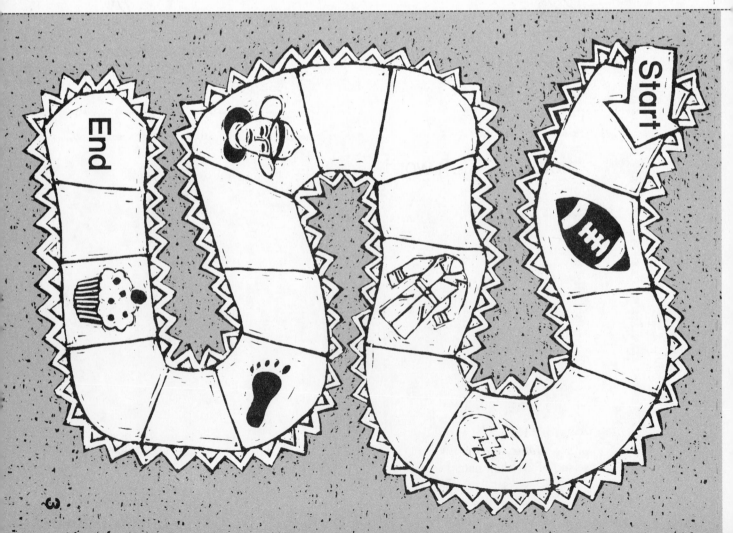

Write a word from the box to match each picture.
Circle the word if it ends like **baby**.
Underline the word if it ends like **cry**.

| bunny | fly | puppy |
| city | fry | silly |

The (baby) will cry.

1.

_____

2.

_____

3.

_____

4.

_____

5.

_____

6.

_____

Draw a picture of each word.

7. berry

8. sky

Notes for Home: Your child practiced reading words with the vowel sounds of *y* heard in *baby* or *cry*. **Home Activity:** Encourage your child to draw pictures of things that have the vowel sound of *y* in their names. Ask your child to label the pictures.

Pick a word from the box to finish each sentence.
Write it on the line below the sentence.

football

| backyard | daytime | eggshell | footprint | haircut |

1. I sat in the _____ of my home.
   _____
   - - - - - - - - - - - - - - - - - - -
   _____

2. I painted the _____ .
   _____
   - - - - - - - - - - - - - - - - - - -
   _____

3. _____ is a good time to play.
   _____
   - - - - - - - - - - - - - - - - - - -
   _____

4. Mr. Green gave Bill a _____ .
   _____
   - - - - - - - - - - - - - - - - - - -
   _____

5. I saw a _____ in the mud.
   _____
   - - - - - - - - - - - - - - - - - - -
   _____

Notes for Home: Your child identified and wrote compound words—longer words formed by joining two smaller words. *Home Activity:* Encourage your child to make up sentences using the compound words from the box above.

Pick a word from the box to finish each sentence.
Write it on the line.

| animals | even | heard | most | their |

1. Last night I _____ something outside.

2. I know that _____ live in our backyard.

5. _____ of them come out at night.

4. I can _____ see them if I look outside.

5. I see _____ faces looking at me!

Notes for Home: This week your child is learning to read the words *animals, even, heard, most,* and *their.* **Home Activity:** Work with your child to write a story using these new words. Help your child read the story to you when he or she is done.

Read each story.
Circle the words that tell what the story is about.
Draw a picture to show what the story is about.

1. Jen feeds her cat.   2.
   She takes care of her cat.
   She pets her cat.

   cats and dogs
   food
   Jen and her cat

3. Mike and Todd are friends.   4.
   They play ball.
   They go to the beach.

   friends
   baseball
   the beach

Write a title for this story.

5. Len looks on the shelf.
   He looks in the box.
   He looks for his cap in many places.

_____

- -

_____

Notes for Home: Your child identified the main idea in a story. *Home Activity:* Read a story with your child. Encourage him or her to tell you what the story is all about.

Some **adjectives** tell how many.   <u>**two**</u> tops

Look at the picture.
Pick a word from the box to finish each sentence.
Write it on the line.

| one | two | three | four | five |

_____
- - - - - - - - - - - -
1. There are _____ balls in the box.

_____
- - - - - - - - - - - -
2. I see _____ toy cats on the floor.

_____
- - - - - - - - - - - -
3. The girl is spinning _____ top.

_____
- - - - - - - - - - - -
4. There are _____ boxes of games.

_____
- - - - - - - - - - - -
5. The man stands by _____ dolls.

Notes for Home: Your child wrote adjectives that tell how many. **Home Activity:** Take a walk with your child. Count objects you see on the way and encourage your child to spell the word for each number.

Pick a word from the box to finish each sentence.
Write it on the line.

> animals   even   heard   heavy   most   their

_____
- - - - - - - - - - - - - - - -
1. Many _____ live on my dad's ranch.

_____
- - - - - - - - - - - - - -
2. I _____ the sheep say "baa."

_____
- - - - - - - - - - - - -
3. _____ of our sheep are black.

_____
- - - - - - - - - - - - - - -
4. We cut _____ hair twice a year.

_____
- - - - - - - - - - - - - - -
5. The big sheep are _____ .

_____
- - - - - - - - - - - - - - -
6. Some are _____ as heavy as my dad.

Notes for Home: Your child completed a story using words learned this week.
Home Activity: Encourage your child to write a poem or song using as many of these words as possible.

pi**e**

kn**igh**t

Circle the word for each picture.

1.	2.	3.	4.
	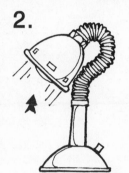		
night note	let light	tie tea	fig fight

5.	6.	7.	8.

pea pie	high hay	sit sigh	tights toads

Find the word that has the same **long i** sound as
Mark the ⬭ to show your answer.

9. ⬭ lit
   ⬭ lie
   ⬭ lift

10. ⬭ mitt
    ⬭ might
    ⬭ mill

Notes for Home: Your child reviewed words in which the long *i* sound is spelled *igh* and *ie* as in *knight* and *pie*. **Home Activity:** Encourage your child to create a poem or song using rhyming *igh* and *ie* words.

Look at each word. **Say** it.
Listen for the **long e** or **long i** sound.

| | Write each word. | Check it. |

1. baby

2. funny

3. many

4. my

5. why

6. fly

Word Wall Words

Write each word.

7. even

8. most

Notes for Home: Your child spelled words in which *y* represents either a long *e* or a long *i* vowel sound, as well as two frequently used words: *even, most.* **Home Activity:** Have your child write and sort the words into long *e* words, long *i* words, and Word Wall Words.

Pick the adjective from the box that tells how many.
Write it on the line.
Draw a line from the group of
words to the picture it matches.

one   two   three   four

1. _____ dolls

2. _____ dog

3. _____ boxes

4. _____ dishes

5.

6.

7.

8.

Draw a picture about six mice.
Write a sentence that tells about your picture.

9.

10. _____

Notes for Home: Your child used adjectives that describe numbers. **_Home Activity:_** Write the numbers 1–10 on a sheet of paper. Ask your child to write the word for each number, then draw a picture to match that number, such as a picture of two cats to go with the number *two*.

Test-Taking Tips

1. Write your name on the test.

2. Read each question twice.

3. Read all the answer choices for the question.

4. Mark your answer carefully.

5. Check your answer.

© Scott Foresman 1

Name _____

Part I: Vocabulary

Read each sentence.

Mark the ⬭ for the word that fits.

_____

1. Sam likes _____.
   ⬭ animals   ⬭ found   ⬭ think

2. He _____ likes bugs!
   ⬭ around   ⬭ together   ⬭ even

3. One day he _____ some ducks.
   ⬭ show   ⬭ bring   ⬭ heard

4. _____ ducks live by the water.
   ⬭ Most   ⬭ About   ⬭ When

5. Sam found _____ nest.
   ⬭ as   ⬭ their   ⬭ more

Part 2: Comprehension

Read each sentence.

Mark the ⬭ for the answer.

6. Dinosaur hunters can
   - ⬭ hear baby dinosaurs.
   - ⬭ see dinosaur mothers.
   - ⬭ find dinosaur eggs.

7. What did some baby dinosaurs eat?
   - ⬭ bugs
   - ⬭ milk
   - ⬭ hot dogs

8. Some big dinosaurs stayed around the baby dinosaurs to
   - ⬭ keep the little ones safe.
   - ⬭ tell a story.
   - ⬭ go to sleep.

9. How were baby dinosaurs like you when you were a baby?
   - ⬭ They were born with teeth.
   - ⬭ They came out of eggs.
   - ⬭ They started growing.

10. What is *Dinosaur Babies* about?
    - ⬭ animals of long ago
    - ⬭ how to eat eggs
    - ⬭ funny tails

Level 1.5

Name _____

Add -ed and **-ing** to each word.
Write the new word on the line.

fix**ing**   fix**ed**

Word		Add -ed	Add -ing
help	1.	_____	2. _____
jog	3.	_____	4. _____
mix	5.	_____	6. _____
hop	7.	_____	8. _____

Find the word that changes its spelling before adding **-ed** or **-ing**.
Mark the ⬭ to show your answer.

9. ⬭ stop   10. ⬭ play
   ⬭ sail   ⬭ snap
   ⬭ talk   ⬭ ask

Notes for Home: Your child added -ed and -ing to verbs, doubling the consonant as needed.
Home Activity: Have your child read aloud the words with -ed and -ing endings. Talk about whether the spelling changed before the endings were added.

baby   funny   many   my   why   fly

Write three words from the box that have the **long e** sound.

1. _____   2. _____   3. _____

Write three words from the box that have the **long i** sound.

4. _____   5. _____   6. _____

Pick a word from the box to match each clue.
Write it in the puzzle.

7. go in plane

8. a lot

Pick a word from the box to finish each sentence.
Write it on the line.

even   most

9. I did _____ of my tasks.

10. I _____ made my bed!

Notes for Home: Your child spelled words in which *y* represents either a long *e* or a long *i* vowel sound, as well as two frequently used words: *even, most.* **Home Activity:** Challenge your child to write other long *e* and long *i* words with *y*.

80 Spelling: Vowel *y:* Long *e* and Long *i* Sounds   Level 1.5

Family Times

The True Story of Abbie Burgess

The Bravest Cat!

Bluey and Dewey

Bluey is a bluebird.
One day he crashes down.
Dewey dashes over
And looks with a frown.

Up in the branches
Bluey hurt his wing.
Dewey helps Bluey
And fixes him a sling.

Dewey teaches Bluey
To fly away.
He wishes he'll see Bluey
On another day.

This rhyme includes words your child is working with in school: words with *ew* and *ue* (*Dewey*, *Bluey*) and words that end in *-es* (*teaches*, *branches*). Chant "Bluey and Dewey" together. Help your child act out the rhyme.

(fold here)

Name: _____

You are your child's first and best teacher!

Here are ways to help your child practice skills while having fun!

Day 1 Work with your child to write notes to friends using as many *ew* and *ue* words as possible. Some words that might be used are: *stew, chew, blew, new, flew, clue,* and *glue.*

Day 2 Help your child write sentences using at least two of the following words in each sentence: *because, better, give, people,* and *put.*

Day 3 Read a story or watch a favorite TV show or video with your child. Encourage your child to tell what happened (effect) and why it happened (cause).

Day 4 Your child is learning to work in small groups. Invite a few friends or family members to join you and your child in a project, such as making cookies or painting pictures.

Day 5 Help your child find information about a topic of interest. Then encourage him or her to write a paragraph explaining what he or she has learned about that topic.

Read with your child EVERY DAY!

4

Mix and Match Plurals

Game Directions

Materials index cards

1. Write the pairs of words shown on page 3 on separate index cards.

2. Mix the cards. Divide them among 2 or 4 players.

3. Players place their cards in a stack and begin flipping over the cards one at a time so all players can see the cards.

4. When a player sees any singular/plural match, he or she yells "Match!" and gets to keep that pair.

5. Play until all matches have been made. The player with the most matches wins!

box	boxes
fox	foxes
dish	dishes
coach	coaches
watch	watches
catch	catches
wish	wishes
crash	crashes
wash	washes
teach	teaches

Name _____

Read the name of each child below.
Pick words from the box with vowel
sounds that are spelled the same.
Write the words on the lines.

 n<u>ew</u>s gl<u>ue</u>

| blue | chew | clue | few | glue | grew | knew | true |

Sue

1. _____

2. _____

3. _____

4. _____

Stewart

5. _____

6. _____

7. _____

8. _____

© Scott Foresman 1

Notes for Home: Your child practiced writing words with the vowel patterns *ew* and *ue*.
Home Activity: Help your child think of other ways to spell the sound made by *ew* and *ue*.

Add -es to the word in ( ) to finish each sentence.
Write the new word on the line.

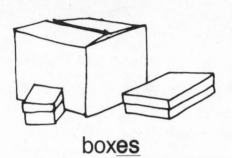

box**es**

She wash**es** the windows

_____ (fox)
- - - - - - - - - - - - - - - -
1. Look at those _____ !

_____ (dish)
- - - - - - - - - - - - - - - -
2. Hand me four _____ .

_____ (bus)
- - - - - - - - - - - - - - - -
3. They took two _____ .

_____ (pass)
- - - - - - - - - - - - - - - -
4. He _____ the ball.

_____ (catch)
- - - - - - - - - - - - - - - -
5. She _____ the ball.

Notes for Home: Your child practiced writing verbs and plural nouns that end in -es.
Home Activity: Write two nouns for your child. Ask your child to point out which ones take
-es to form a plural. (Nouns that end in s, ss, sh, ch, and x use -es when made plural.)

Name _____

Pick a word from the box to finish each sentence.
Write it on the line.

because	better	give	people	put

_____

1. I like to ride my bike _____ it is fun.

_____

2. Some _____ like skating.

_____

3. I like riding _____ than skating.

_____

4. I _____ my baby sister a ride!

_____

5. I always _____ my bike away.

Notes for Home: This week your child is learning to read the words *because, better, give, people*, and *put*. **Home Activity:** Write each word on a separate slip of paper. Put the slips of paper in a bowl or hat. Ask your child to pick one word and use it in a sentence.

© Scott Foresman 1

Draw a line to match what happens with why it happens.

What Happens	**Why It Happens**

1.

2.

3.

4.

5.

 Notes for Home: Your child identified what happens (effect) and why it happens (cause).
Home Activity: While watching a television show, encourage your child to identify what happens and why.

An **adjective** tells more about a person, place, or thing.
Cute tells more about Mary's cat.

Mary has a **<u>cute</u>** cat.

Pick a word from the box that helps each sentence tell more.
Write it on the line.

| black | hot | tall | three | wet |

1. Dad sips a _____ drink.

2. Tom is a _____ man.

3. I have a _____ cat.

4. I have _____ sisters.

5. Take off your _____ coat.

Notes for Home: Your child used adjectives to improve sentences. *Home Activity:* Make up simple sentences for your child. Encourage your child to add adjectives to make each sentence more interesting.

Name _____

Pick a word from the box to finish each sentence.
Write it on the line.

because	better	burns	give	people	put

_____

1. My dog barks _____ there is a fire!

_____

2. His barking wakes up the sleeping _____ .

_____

3. The firefighters _____ the fire out.

_____

4. My dog has _____ on his feet.

_____

5. I will _____ my dog a big hug.

_____

6. That will make him feel _____ .

Notes for Home: Your child used words learned this week to finish a story. *Home Activity:*
Take turns reading each word from the box aloud and using it in a sentence.

fr**y**

bab**y**

Circle the word for each picture.

1. many   man

2. sit   city

3. lock   lucky

4. carry   care

5. funny   fry

6. cry   crib

7. flea   fly

8. sky   skate

Find the word where **y** does **not** have the same sound as the other two words.

Mark the ⬭ to show your answer.

9. ⬭ my
   ⬭ many
   ⬭ Mary

10. ⬭ why
    ⬭ spy
    ⬭ lady

Notes for Home: Your child reviewed the vowel sounds of *y*—the long *e* sound in *baby* and the long *i* sound in *fry*. **Home Activity:** Work with your child to write two word lists—one of words in which *y* represents the long *e* sound and one in which it represents the long *i* sound.

Name _____

Look at each word. **Say** it.
Listen for the vowel sound.

Write each word.   **Check** it.

1. new

2. grew

3. drew

4. blue

5. true

6. glue

Word Wall Words

Write each word.

7. give

8. put

Notes for Home: Your child spelled words with *ew* and *ue* that stand for the same vowel sound, as well as two frequently used words: *give, put.* **Home Activity:** Encourage your child to draw pictures for some of the spelling words. Help your child label each picture.

90 Spelling: Vowels *ue, ew* /ü/   **Level 1.5**

Add adjectives to tell more about a person, place, or thing.

Jan has a dog.   Jan has a **small** dog.

What word describes the animal best?
Circle a word to finish each sentence.
Write it on the line.

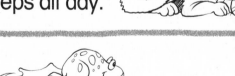

old   bushy   new
_____

1. The pup has a _____ tail.

long   sweet   nice
_____

2. What _____ legs the spider has!

square   shy   best
_____

3. The _____ mice hide in their cage.

fast   fine   lazy
_____

4. The _____ cat sleeps all day.

Write about a frog.
Use an adjective to describe it.

_____

5. _____

Notes for Home: Your child used adjectives (words that describe a person, place, or thing) to improve sentences. ***Home Activity:*** Write some simple sentences for your child. *(I saw a cow.)* Invite your child to improve the sentences with one or more adjectives. *(I saw a big, fat cow.)*

Name _____

Look at the picture.
Circle the adjective that tells more about the picture.

new   old

1. The _____ home was on fire.

strong   weak

2. A _____ cat walked out.

striped   spotted

3. It was carrying a _____ kitten.

little   huge

4. The _____ kitten was now safe.

Write a sentence about the cat in the picture.
Use an adjective from the box.   big   brave   older   glad

_____

5. _____

_____

Notes for Home: Your child used adjectives to make sentences more descriptive. **Home Activity:** Say a simple sentence naming an object around you *(I see a tree.)*. Encourage your child to improve your sentence by adding adjectives to it *(I see a tall, green tree.)*.

Part 1: Vocabulary

Read each sentence.
Mark the ⬭ for the word that fits.

1. Some _____ saw a fire.
   ⬭ please   ⬭ every   ⬭ people

2. They _____ out the fire.
   ⬭ come   ⬭ put   ⬭ play

3. The tree has _____ on it.
   ⬭ only   ⬭ burns   ⬭ better

4. It will not get _____ .
   ⬭ around   ⬭ better   ⬭ because

5. The man will _____ us a new tree.
   ⬭ give   ⬭ put   ⬭ sing

GO ON ➡

Part 2: Comprehension

Read each question.
Mark the ⬯ for the answer.

6. What building was on fire?
   - ⬯ a shop
   - ⬯ a garage
   - ⬯ a hospital

7. Why did the cat run into the fire?
   - ⬯ to put the fire out
   - ⬯ to get her kittens
   - ⬯ to help the people

8. The mother cat could not see her kittens because
   - ⬯ the fire hurt her eyes.
   - ⬯ a man took the kittens away.
   - ⬯ the kittens were in a box.

9. How were Karen Wellen and Scarlett alike?
   - ⬯ They ran in and out to get the kittens.
   - ⬯ They went to sleep in the garage.
   - ⬯ They took a long time to get better.

10. *The Bravest Cat!* tells about a
    - ⬯ real cat.
    - ⬯ cat that sings.
    - ⬯ funny cat.

Name _____

lu**ng**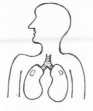

ba**nk**

Circle the word for each picture.

1. 	**2.** 	**3.** 	**4.** 
tank tan	rink ring	fang fan	skunk skate
5. 	**6.** 	**7.** 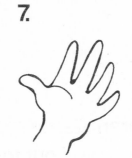	**8.** 
drip drink	sign sing	hand hung	kin ink

Find the word that has the same ending sound as .
Mark the ⬭ to show your answer.

9. ⬭ sand
⬭ sang
⬭ sank

10. ⬭ train
⬭ think
⬭ thing

 Notes for Home: Your child reviewed words that end with *-ng* and *-nk*. **Home Activity:** Say one of the words with *-ing* or *-nk* on this page and ask your child to think of a word that rhymes with it. Then have your child think of a word for you to rhyme.

Name _____

new   grew   drew   blue   true   glue

Write three words from the box that end with **ue**.

_____   _____   _____

1. _____   2. _____   3. _____

Write three words from the box that end with **ew**.

_____   _____   _____

4. _____   5. _____   6. _____

Write the words from the box that tell something that happened in the past.

_____   _____

7. _____   8. _____

Pick a word from the box to finish each sentence.
Write it on the line.

give   put

_____

9. _____ me the cat.

_____

10. I will _____ him in his bed.

Notes for Home: Your child spelled words with *ew* and *ue* that stand for the same vowel sound, as well as two frequently used words: *give, put*. **Home Activity:** Work with your child to write the spelling words in alphabetical order.

96 Spelling: Vowels *ue, ew* /ü/   Level 1.5

Name _____

Correct each sentence.

Write it on the line.

Hint: Each sentence should begin with a capital letter.

It should end with a . or ? .

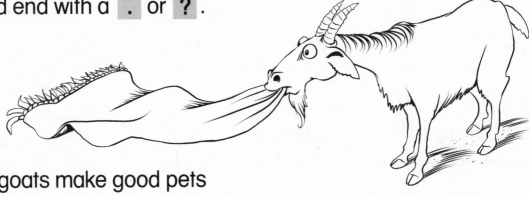

1. do goats make good pets

_____

- -

_____

2. we had a goat named Jo

_____

- -

_____

3. it liked to come inside

_____

- -

_____

4. one day it ate a rug

_____

- -

_____

5. why do goats like rugs

_____

- -

_____

Notes for Home: Your child corrected sentences using capital letters and end marks. ***Home Activity:*** Help your child find out about a favorite animal. Invite your child to write a short report on that animal. Make sure that sentences are written correctly.

Name _____

I read _____
_____
_____

It was about

Words I Can Now Read and Write

_____

_____

I read _____

_____

_____

It was about

Words I Can Now Read and Write

_____   _____

_____   _____

_____   _____

Words I Can Now Read and Write

I read _____

_____

It was about

Words I Can Now Read and Write

_____   _____

_____   _____

Words I Can Now Read and Write

_____ _____
- - - - - - - - - - - - - - - - - - - - - - - - - - - - - - - -
_____ _____

_____ _____
- - - - - - - - - - - - - - - - - - - - - - - - - - - - - - - -
_____ _____

_____ _____
- - - - - - - - - - - - - - - - - - - - - - - - - - - - - - - -
_____ _____

_____ _____
- - - - - - - - - - - - - - - - - - - - - - - - - - - - - - - -
_____

_____
- - - - - - - - - - - - - - - -
_____

_____
- - - - - - - - - - - - - - - -
_____

Name _____

_____

I read _____

_____

_ _

_____

It was about

Words I Can Now Read and Write

_____   _____
_ _ _ _ _ _ _ _ _ _ _ _   _ _ _ _ _ _ _ _ _ _ _ _
_____   _____
_ _ _ _ _ _ _ _ _ _ _ _   _ _ _ _ _ _ _ _ _ _ _ _
_____   _____

Words I Can Now Read and Write

Name _____

I read _____

_____

_____

It was about

Words I Can Now Read and Write

_____   _____

_____   _____

_____   _____

Name _____

Words I Can Now Read and Write

Name _____

I read _____

_____

It was about

Words I Can Now Read and Write

_____   _____

_____   _____

Name _____

Words I Can Now Read and Write